D0601273

Country Music

Published by Creative Education
P.O. Box 227
Mankato, Minnesota 56002
Creative Education is an imprint of The Creative Company.

design and production by ZENO DESIGN

photographs by Corbis (Bettmann; Kevin Fleming; James Lance; Neal Preston;
Bob Sacha; Bradley Smith), Getty Images (Thomas D. McAvoy/Time Life
Pictures; Michael Ochs Archives; Ralph Notaro)

Copyright © 2008 Creative Education.
International copyright reserved in all countries.
No part of this book may be reproduced in any form
without written permission from the publisher.
Printed in the United States of America

LIBRARY OF CONGRESS CATALOGING-IN-PUBLICATION DATA

Riggs, Kate.
Country music / by Kate Riggs.
p. cm. — (World of music)
Includes index.
isbn 978-1-58341-565-8
1. Country music—History and criticism—Juvenile literature. I. Title.

ML3524.R54 2008
781.642—dc22   2006102982

First edition

9 8 7 6 5 4 3 2 1

Country

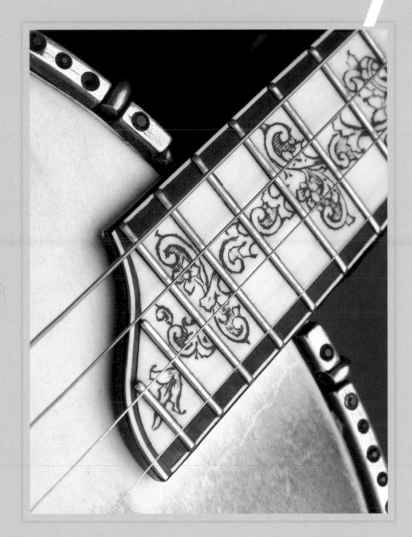

MUSIC

KATE RIGGS

Mamie Doud Eisenhower
Public Library
Broomfield, CO 80020

Withdrawn

MAR 2 0 2008

creative ● education

Country music is an old kind of music. It started more than 200 years ago. People moved to the United States from lots of different places. They made up songs to tell stories about their lives. They sang the songs to each other.

The first country singers sang songs called ballads.

Country music is for people of all ages

The Carter Family was a country music group. They were one of the first famous groups. They sang lots of fun songs. They played string instruments called guitars, too.

The Carter Family recorded more than 300 songs together!

The Carter Family of the 1950s

A man named Gene Autry (*AH-tree*) was a country singer, too. He sang songs like cowboys used to sing. People liked his cowboy songs. Some of his songs had funny sounds in them. He said things like "yippee-ki-yi-yay." He wanted to sound like a real cowboy.

Singer Gene Autry had lots of fans

Cowboys played guitars when they sang. So Gene Autry played a guitar, too. People called him the "Singing Cowboy."

Gene Autry wore a white cowboy hat wherever he went.

A guitar used in playing country music

Soon, people got tired of cowboy songs. They wanted to hear different kinds of songs. So they started a new kind of country music. It was called bluegrass.

A bluegrass band playing on a stage

Bluegrass singers did not play only guitars. They played fiddles and banjos, too. A violin is called a "fiddle" in bluegrass music. Banjos can make fast, fun sounds. Fiddles can make lots of fun sounds, too!

A guitar has six strings. Most country singers use guitars.

Singer Keith Urban plays banjo sometimes

Johnny Cash made new sounds in country music with his deep voice. Willie Nelson made new sounds, too. Some of their songs sounded angry. Other songs sounded sad. Lots of people liked the new sounds.

Johnny Cash always wore black clothes. He was called "The Man in Black."

Willie Nelson still sings all over the U.S.

Faith Hill is a country singer today. Lots of people like her pretty voice. They like her fun stories, too. She sings songs about people she knows. She sings songs about people she does not know, too.

Faith Hill became a big country star in 1993

Some country music is fast. Some is slow. Lots of people like country music. It tells the stories of different people.

"Always on My Mind" is a famous song by Willie Nelson.

Shania Twain is a popular country singer

GLOSSARY

ballads long, sad songs that tell stories about people

banjos instruments that people play by picking the strings with their fingers

cowboys men who rode horses and took care of animals

instruments things people play to make music

Some country stars dress like cowboys

INDEX